Bats

By Debbie Croft

Fin has a bat.

Fin can see the net.

Fin can tap to Sam!

Tip, tap, tip, tap!

Fin

Sam

net

bat

3

Tam is fit.

She has a bat.

Tam can hit.

Bam! Bam!

Tam

bat

It is Tim.

Tim has a bat.

Tim hits and hits!

Tim

bat

A bat!

It can sip.

CHECKING FOR MEANING

1. Who is tapping the ball over the net? *(Literal)*

2. What sound does it make when Tam hits the ball with the bat? *(Literal)*

3. What is the bat sipping on page 9? *(Inferential)*

EXTENDING VOCABULARY

bat	What other words rhyme with *bat*? Take off the *b* and put another letter in its place to make a new word, e.g. mat, cat, sat.
net	Explain the meaning of *net* in this text. Where else could you see a net?
Bam	Find words in the text that are used for the sounds made by using a bat. Explain why these words are written in a different font.

MOVING BEYOND THE TEXT

1. Why are the sports bats different shapes?

2. What materials are the sports bats made from? Are they all the same?

3. Make a list of sports for which players use a bat.

4. What is the difference between the bats used to hit balls and the bat on page 9?

SPEED SOUNDS

Cc	Bb	Rr	Ee	Ff	Hh	Nn

Mm	Ss	Aa	Pp	Ii	Tt

PRACTICE WORDS

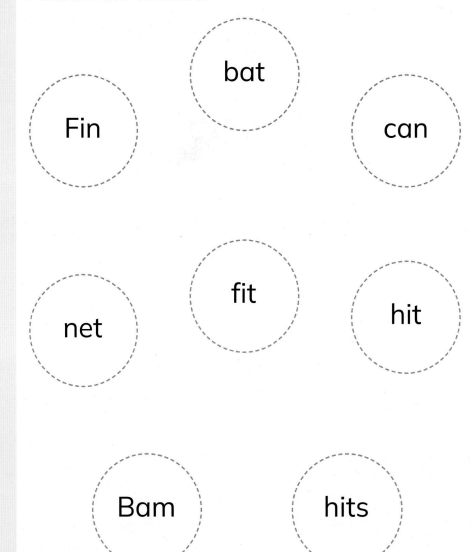

bat

Fin

can

fit

net

hit

Bam

hits